Mister Skellybones

by Douglas Wootton
edited by Alison Hedger

A humorous short musical exploring the wonderful human body

Suitable for KEY STAGE 1
although the appealing songs will be enjoyed by all ages!

Duration approximately 30 minutes

TEACHER'S BOOK complete with play, lyrics, music and matching CD of all the music
in the show. Backing tracks are included for performances and rehearsal,
as well as the complete songs for learning purposes.

SONGS

1. Who Can It Be?
2. In The Mirror
3. Each Little Finger
4. The Skeleton Rock
5. Here's My Tummy
6. Everybody's Happy When They're Dancing
7. Captain Heart And Doctor Brain

© Copyright 2000 Golden Apple Productions
A division of Chester Music Limited
8/9 Frith Street, London W1V 5TZ

Order No. GA11106

ISBN 0-7119-7921-9

CAST AND COSTUMES

Mister Skellybones*
The Skelly Tones,
musical skeletons
(three to speak)
} Black jumpers and tights with white bones painted onto clothing. Luminous paint is fun if using stage lighting.

Children
(some to speak solo)
T shirts, shorts and bare feet, some of the children could have baking foil attached to T shirts to represent mirrors, ready for working in pairs

Captain Heart
Mainly red, military-type hat

Doctor Brain
White coat and stethoscope

*(Mister Skellybones can be "cloned", or have a Miss Skellybones wearing perhaps a tu-tu skirt and beads. The words for Mister Skellybones can then be allocated to others should this be too demanding for one child. Alternatively, perhaps a member of staff could be Mister Skellybones?)

OPTIONAL PROPS

- Mirror(s) - only pretend! Hand held or free standing (see above)

- Cardboard cut-outs of food and bin liners into which children drop their "food" (Song 5). The bag can be shaken to represent digestion!

- Consider having a life size (or larger) picture of a skeleton, and alongside a human body in trunks. These could be your backdrop and be pointed to at relevant times. The human figure could have a large open mouth, with a bin liner behind to catch food as children "feed" their cardboard food.

MOVEMENT

Actions follow the song words. A well-rehearsed action routine is always fun to do and to watch. The happy, snappy music will naturally set feet a-tapping! Make as much of the dances as talent and space allows.

SONGS

You may care to divide the song lyrics between groups or solos. Otherwise, everyone can sing together, which will work well.

MISTER SKELLYBONES

All children and skeletons are on stage in suitable positions for dialogue between them. Captain Heart and Doctor Brain are best kept out of direct view, so that their appearance later has maximum effect.

Mister Skellybones addresses both children and the audience.

Mister Skellybones (*In rap style*)	Hi there everybody, I'm Mister Skellybones It's great to see you here to meet My friends the Skelly Tones. (*gesture*)
All Skelly Tones	(*hum a note*)
1st Skeleton	We've got a little show, About the things we know –
2nd Skeleton	About the human body. How it works and how we grow.
3rd Skeleton (*to children*)	Now, when you look into a mirror what <u>do</u> you see?
All Children	Why somebody of course who looks <u>just like Me</u>!
Mister Skellybones	Woh! Then show me bro'!

Select some children to do mirror actions before song, then sing.

SONG ONE   WHO CAN IT BE?

Who can it be, who can it be,
This person who looks just like me?
Who can it be, who can it be?
There's someone who can copy me!
And wave at me –
(*wave*)
Jump like me –
(*jump*)
And clap, clap, clap their hands like me.
(*clap*)
And smile like me –
(*smile*)
Nod like me –
(*nod*)
And tap, tap, tap their feet like me.
(*tap*)
Who can it be, who can it be,
This person who looks just like me?
Who can it be, who can it be?
There's someone who can copy,
Copy, copy, copy,
Someone who can copy me!

Repeat whole song for a dance with mirrored actions

A free-standing "mirror" can be brought onto the stage, or children can look into hand-held "mirrors", or look at partner's T shirt "mirror". (See Production notes)

Mister Skellybones   OK so let's start at the top.
                          Now, what <u>else</u> do you see?

All children   I can see my face and it's looking back at me!

SONG TWO   IN THE MIRROR

**In the mirror I can see
My face looking back at me.
Two eyes that open wide and close,
And in the middle here's my nose.**

**In the mirror I can see
My face looking back at me.
And on each side I've got an ear,
And they are there so I can hear.**

**In the mirror I can see
My face looking back at me.
My mouth that I can open wide,
And I can see my tongue inside!**

**My eyes to see, my nose to smell,
My ears to hear you really well.
My mouth to say the words I've said.
All these things are on my head.**

Mister Skellybones   Now let me see you scratch your head –
                          How are you going to do it?
                          Of course you use your fingers . . . (*all scratch*)
                          There's really nothing to it.

A skeleton   Hold your hands up in the air
                          And wiggle all your fingers there.

SONG THREE   EACH LITTLE FINGER

1.   **Each little finger wiggles like this,
            Wiggles like this, wiggles like this.
            Each little finger wiggles like this on my hands
            At the end of my wrists, my wrists.
            This is my wrist, this is my wrist,** (*Hold right wrist then left wrist*)
            It helps my hand to wave and twist.

2.   **Both of my arms can hug you so tight,
            Hug you so tight, hug you so tight.
            Both of my arms can hug you so tight –
            When I hug you it feels just right, just right.
            My arms can stretch and pull and tug,
            But most of all they like to HUG!** (*Hug yourself!*)

4

Child	Oh Mister Skellybones you are so very bony, Your arms and legs and fingers are like sticks of macaroni.
Child	Is <u>that</u> what's underneath our skin? Our skin that keeps our insides in? Those bones so hard and knobbly!
Child	I suppose without our skeletons We'd be all weak and wobbly.
A skeleton	Well that is absolutely right, Without your bones you'd be a sight!
A skeleton	So <u>we're</u> gonna sing you a rock 'n' roll song All about your marvellous skeleton.
A skeleton	Get your blue suede shoes and your party frock 'Cause we're all gonna boogie to *The Skeleton Rock*!

SONG FOUR   THE SKELETON ROCK

1.

Now I'm gonna tell you 'bout a wonderful thing.
It's all about them bones that's underneath your skin.
So come on everybody clap your hands and sing.
We're gonna dance to the skeleton rock.

Refrain

We're gonna dance, dance, dance,
Dance to the skeleton, dance to the skeleton rock.
When you hear them bones a-rattle, tic-tac-toc!
We're gonna dance to the skeleton rock!

} *twice*

2.

Now we all need a skeleton to keep our shape,
Because without our bones we couldn't stand up straight.
Just imagine how wob-b-ly we all would be.
Like jellyfish swimming under the sea.

Refrain

We're gonna dance, dance, dance,
Dance to the skeleton, dance to the skeleton rock.
When you hear them bones a-rattle tic-tac-toc!
We're gonna dance to the skeleton rock!
We're gonna dance, dance, dance,
Dance to the skeleton, dance to the skeleton rock.
When you hear them bones a-rattle, tic-tac-toc!
We're gonna dance to the skeleton
Dance to the skeleton,
Dance to the skeleton rock!

All children

But if you want your body,
To grow up straight and tall,
You have to eat your food up,
You have to eat it <u>all</u>!

So next time that your mummy,
Makes you something really yummy
Be sure that every little bit,
Goes down into your tummy!

SONG FIVE   HERE'S MY TUMMY

1. Here's my tummy, here's my tummy,
   Where my food goes if it's yummy. } *twice*
   Chicken nuggets, loads of chips,
   Pizza, sausages and crisps.
   Down they go into my tum.
   Lots of lovely food, yum-yum!

2. Here's my tummy, here's my tummy,
   Where my food goes if it's yummy. } *twice*
   Lots of lovely fruit to share,
   Apples, oranges and pears.
   Down they go into my tum.
   Lots of lovely food, yum-yum!

3. Here's my tummy, here's my tummy,
   Where my food goes if it's yummy. } *twice*
   Vegetables are tasty too,
   And they're very good for you.
   Down they go into my tum,
   Lots of lovely food yum-yum!

All children

Down below your tummy
Are two long things with knees.
They help you walk along the street
And wobble when you sneeze.

And on the end so very neat
Two pitter-patter dancing feet.
My legs are very pleased to have
Such lovely feet as these!

Children who will dance take their partner's hands ready for next song

SONG SIX   EVERYBODY'S HAPPY WHEN THEY'RE DANCING

1.2.&3.

Legs are made to walk,
Legs are made to run,
Feet are made for dancing
So that we can have fun.
Take your partner's hand,
Round and round we go.
Everybody's happy
When they're dancing you know.

(1.) Touch the ground,
Turn around.
Whistle if you can 'cause
It's a wonderful sound.

(2.) Point your toe,
Take a bow.
You can click your fingers
If you think you know how.

(3.) Clap your hands,
Shout hooray!
Wave at everyone to
Show you're happy today.

Take your partner's hand,
Round and round we go.
Everybody's happy
When they're dancing you know.

Child	So these are our bodies, Our bodies are us,
Child	But what makes them work With so little fuss?
Child	How do we lift and carry and throw? What makes us think and what makes us go?
Mister Skellybones	Well just before we end our show, Here are two friends you ought to know. So clap your hands and sing again – It's Captain Heart and Doctor Brain.

SONG SEVEN CAPTAIN HEART AND DOCTOR BRAIN

Refrain **Captain Heart and Doctor Brain,**
We're the ones who take the strain. } *twice*

1. **Doctor Brain he tells you how**
To do the things you're doing now.
He helps you think and write and read,
He's got the answers that you need.
Your own computer in your head,
He even works when you're in bed!

Refrain **Captain Heart and Doctor Brain . . .**

2. **Captain Heart she does her best,**
She thumps away inside your chest.
She's pumping all the blood around,
To keep your body fit and sound.
So when you want to run and jump,
Just feel how hard she has to pump.

Refrain **Captain Heart and Doctor Brain**
We're the ones who take the strain. } *twice*
Yeah!

Child	But now it's <u>really</u> time to go, We hope you have enjoyed our show.
Child	But, if you want to find out more About this body we call ME,
All	You'll have to go and get a book about ANATOMY! BYE BYE!

Repeat Song 4 Skeleton Rock for finale.

SONG ONE WHO CAN IT BE?

Repeat for a dance

SONG TWO IN THE MIRROR

Yr 1
3/9.

1. Each lit - tle fin - ger

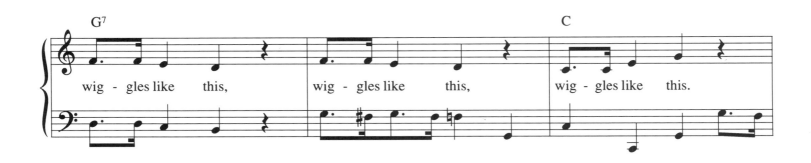

wig - gles like this, wig - gles like this, wig - gles like this.

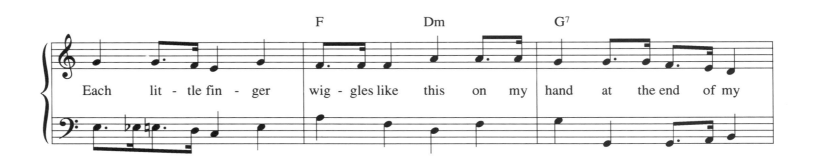

Each lit - tle fin - ger wig - gles like this on my hand at the end of my

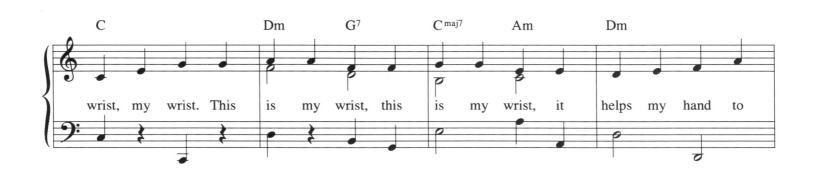

wrist, my wrist. This is my wrist, this is my wrist, it helps my hand to

SONG FOUR THE SKELETON ROCK

Speed ♩ = 140

I'm gon - na tell you 'bout a won - der - ful thing. It's all a -
(2.) all need a ske - le - ton to keep our shape, be - cause with -

- bout them bones that's un - der - neath your skin. So come
- out our bones we could - n't stand up straight. Just im -

on ev - ery - bod - y clap your hands and sing. We're gon - na
- ag - ine how wob - b - ly we all would be. Like jel - ly

dance to the ske - le - ton rock. We're gon - na
fish swim - ming un - der the sea.

Refrain

SONG FIVE HERE'S MY TUMMY

Speed ♩ = 132–140

(no chords)

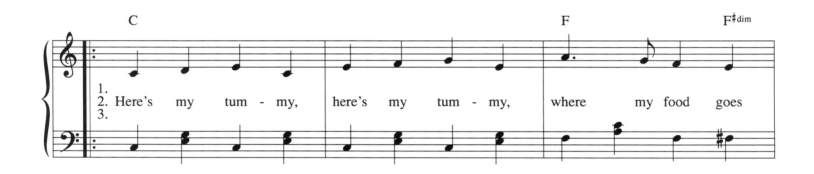

1.
2. Here's my tum - my, here's my tum - my, where my food goes

3.

if it's yum - my. Here's my tum - my, here's my tum - my,

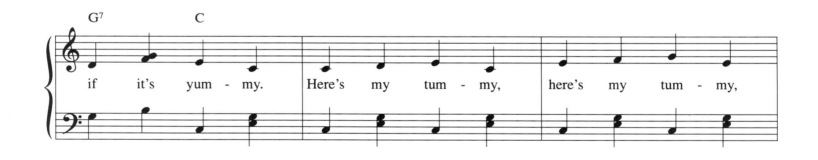

where my food goes if it's yum - my.

Chick - en nug - gets,
Lots of love - ly
Vege - ta - bles are

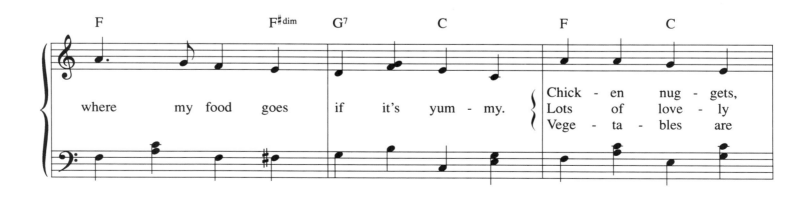

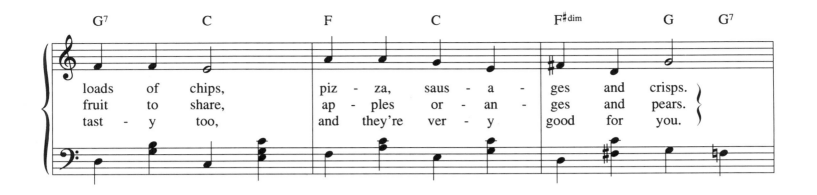

loads of chips, pizza, saus-a-ges and crisps.
fruit to share, ap-ples or-an-ges and pears.
tast-y too, and they're ver-y good for you.

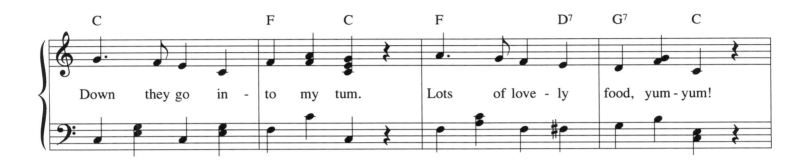

Down they go in-to my tum. Lots of love-ly food, yum-yum!

to continue

to finish

EVERYBODY'S HAPPY WHEN THEY'RE DANCING

Touch the ground,___ turn a - round.___
Point your toe,___ take a bow.___
Clap your hands,___ shout hoo - ray!___

Whis - tle if you can 'cause it's a won - der - ful sound.___
You can click your fin - gers if you think you know how.___
Wave at eve - ry - one to show you're hap - py to - day.___

1.2.

Take your part - ner's hand, round and round we go.

Ev - ery - bod - y's hap - py when they're danc - ing you know.___

(good place to change partners)

turn over for 3rd time bars

19

3. F

Take your part - ner's hand, round and round we go.

B♭   F/C   G⁷   C⁷ᵃᵈᵈ⁴   F

Ev - ery - bo - dy's hap - py when they're danc - ing____ you____ know.

CAPTAIN HEART AND DOCTOR BRAIN

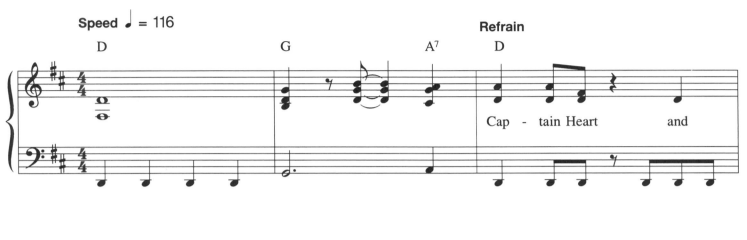

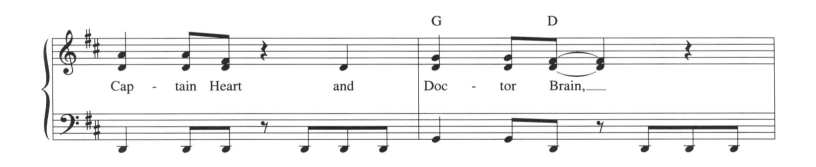

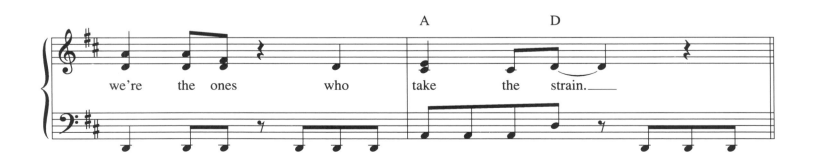

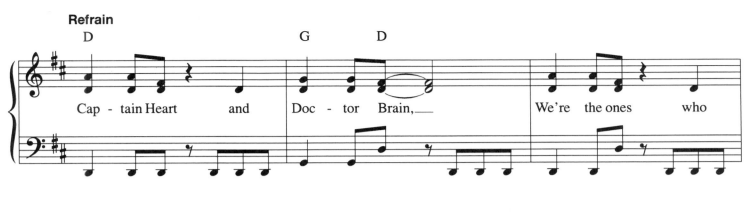

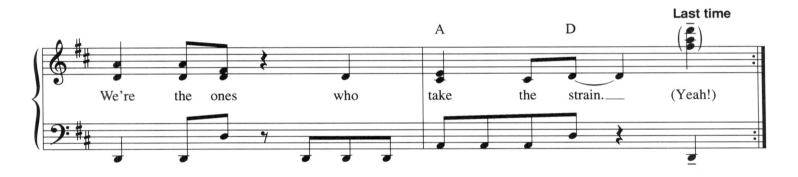

Golden Apple Key Stage One Music for every season

The Musicians Of Bremen

A fun, short musical play based on the popular story by the Brothers Grimm. Ideal for class or year productions. Written by Sheila Wainwright, with music by Alison Hedger.

Teacher's Book GA11009
Matching Cassette GA11010

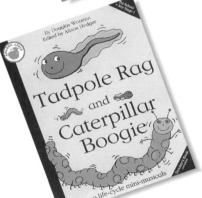

Tadpole Rag And Caterpillar Boogie

Two charming and factual mini-musicals in one book, exploring the life-cycles of frogs and butterflies. Each musical has five easy-to-learn songs linked by rhyming narration, by Douglas Wootton.

Teacher's Book GA11061
Matching Cassette GA11062

Harvest Time!

A fun harvest celebration written by Alison Hedger for schools and Sunday schools with six short new songs. Ideal for involving every child at your school in a meaningful celebration.

Teacher's Book GA11086
Matching Cassette GA11087

Fishing For Stars

A delightful new nativity for younger children based on the traditional Christmas story. Containing six original songs written by Niki Davies.

Teacher's Book GA11088
Matching Cassette GA11089